W9-BFA-326

GEOGRAPHY NOW!

ISLANDS

AROUND THE WORLD

JEN GREEN

PowerKiDS
press.

New York

Published in 2009 by The Rosen Publishing Group Inc.
29 East 21st Street, New York, NY 10010

First Edition

Editor: Jon Richards
Designer: Ben Ruocco
Consultant: John Williams

Library of Congress Cataloging-in-Publication Data

Green, Jen.
  Islands around the world / Jen Green. — 1st ed.
      p. cm. — (Geography now)
  Includes index.
  ISBN 978-1-4358-2872-8 (library binding)
  ISBN 978-1-4358-2958-9 (paperback)
  ISBN 978-1-4358-2964-0 (6-pack)
  1. Islands—Juvenile literature. I. Title.
  GB471.G74 2009
  551.42—dc22

                                    2008025811

Manufactured in China

Picture acknowledgments:
(t-top, b-bottom, l-left, r-right, c-center)
Front cover Dreamstime.com/Wolfgang Amri, 1 istockphoto.com/Martin Maun, 4-5 Dreamstime.com/
Ian Bracegirdle, 4br Dreamstime.com/Mika Makkonen, 5br courtesy of NASA, 6-7 courtesy of NASA, 6bl
Dreamstime.com/Sharpshot, 7br courtesy of NASA, 8-9 courtesy of NASA, 9br Dreamstime.com/Albo, 10-11
Dreamstime.com/Greg Pelt, 10bl Dreamstime.com/David Lloyd, 11br Dreamstime.com/Lior Filshteiner, 12-13
Dreamstime.com/Andrew Chambers, 12bl istockphoto.com/Martin Maun,13bc courtesy of NASA, 13br
courtesy of US Department of Energy, 14-15 istockphoto.com/Alexander Hafemann, 14bl Dreamstime.com/
Gian Marco Valente, 15br Yomangani, 16-17 istockphoto.com/ Rob Broek, 16bl Staffan Widstrand/CORBIS,
17br Erik Torpegaard, 18-19 Dreamstime.com/Gary Hartz, 19cr istockphoto/Kristian Larsen, 19br istockphoto/
Ian Campbell, 20-21 istockphoto.com/Jivko Kazakov, 20bl courtesy of NASA, 21br istockphoto.com/Jiri Vatka,
22-23 istockphoto.com/Joshua Haviv, 22b courtesy of the Library of Congress, 23br courtesy of NASA, 24-25
Wayne Lawler; Ecoscene/CORBIS, 24bl istockphoto.com/Omar Ariff, 25br Dreamstime.com/Bernard Breton,
26-27 Dreamstime.com/Dennis Sabo, 26br istockphoto.com/narvikk, 27br ANURUDDHA
LOKUHAPUARACHCHI/Reuters/Corbis, 28-29 Dreamstime.com/Sitha Suppalertpisit, 28bl
Dreamstime.com/Hans-Thomas Müller, 29br Dreamstime.com/Andy Heyward

CONTENTS

What are islands?

Islands are areas of land completely surrounded by water. Although islands are smaller than continents, some islands are huge, covering many thousands of square miles. Other islands are just dots in the ocean or areas of land found in lakes and rivers.

ISLAND VARIETY

Islands are incredibly diverse. Some have soaring mountains, and others are low and rounded. Some are densely forested, and others are grassy or bare. Islands form in several different ways, but the two main types are called continental and oceanic (see pages 6–9). Some islands are found in groups called archipelagos, and others run in long chains.

Islands such as Hong Kong are home to millions of people. The natural landscape has been transformed by urban development, including high-rise buildings.

Some islands are uninhabited. In the crowded modern world, such places can often be vital refuges for wildlife. This is one of the Whitsunday Islands off the coast of Australia.

ISLAND ENVIRONMENTS

Islands are special places that are often homes to unusual plants and animals. Since ancient times, people have been attracted to islands and have chosen to settle on them—but human settlements have put natural habitats at risk. Today, some of the world's greatest cities, such as New York City and Hong Kong, are located on islands.

Strategic locations

Some islands or island groups, such as Japan, form a separate country. Others, such as Hong Kong, are part of another country (China). New Guinea is divided between nations. Some islands have strategic importance. Malta, for example, has been used as a military base for centuries.

The Mediterranean island of Malta has been claimed by the Arabs, Normans, French, and British at various points in history. It is now the smallest nation in the European Union (EU).

Continental islands

Many of the world's largest islands are continental islands. These islands lie close to mainlands. They rise from the broad, flat ledges that surround the great landmasses, called continental shelves. The waters here are shallow, less than 660 ft. (200 m) deep.

CUT OFF FROM MAINLANDS

Continental islands were once part of mainlands. They were cut off by rising seas or when the land between them sank or subsided. During the last Ice Age, Britain was joined to mainland Europe. During this cold era, sea levels were lower, because a lot of water was frozen. As the climate warmed about 18,000 years ago, ice melted, swelling the oceans. The sea rose and Britain became an island.

Tidal islands, such as St. Michael's Mount in Cornwall, are part-time islands—entirely surrounded by water only at high tide. At low tide, a causeway links the island to the mainland.

MOVING LAND

Some continental islands lie a long way from the nearest continent, separated due to a process called plate tectonics. The Earth's outer crust is made up of a number of huge slabs called tectonic plates. These plates drift very slowly over hot, liquid rock below. Over millions of years, this plate movement carries islands far from the landmasses to which they once belonged.

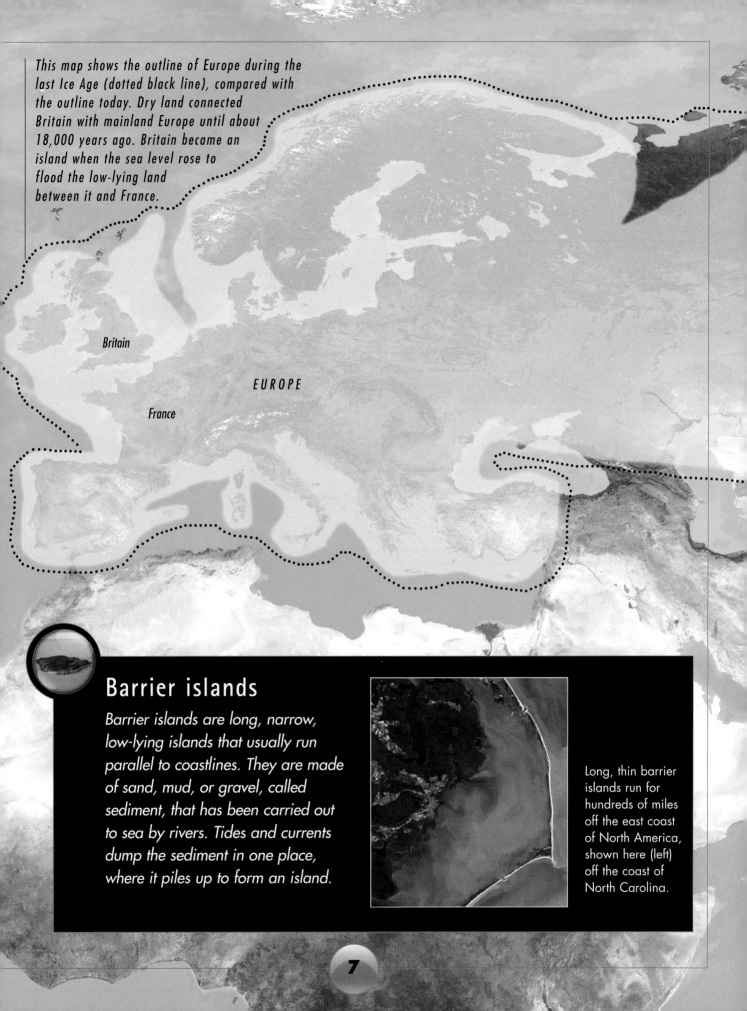

This map shows the outline of Europe during the last Ice Age (dotted black line), compared with the outline today. Dry land connected Britain with mainland Europe until about 18,000 years ago. Britain became an island when the sea level rose to flood the low-lying land between it and France.

Britain

France

EUROPE

Barrier islands

Barrier islands are long, narrow, low-lying islands that usually run parallel to coastlines. They are made of sand, mud, or gravel, called sediment, that has been carried out to sea by rivers. Tides and currents dump the sediment in one place, where it piles up to form an island.

Long, thin barrier islands run for hundreds of miles off the east coast of North America, shown here (left) off the coast of North Carolina.

Oceanic islands

Oceanic islands are usually small. They have never been connected to a continent, and often lie far out in the open sea. Many oceanic islands are the tops of underwater volcanoes and are made from a volcanic rock called basalt.

Most volcanic islands rise from the sea near the borders of tectonic plates, but the islands of Hawaii lie at a point called a hot spot, in the middle of a tectonic plate.

PILES OF LAVA

Most oceanic islands formed as a result of volcanic activity. They began life when molten rock from deep underground erupted from cracks in the seabed. As time went on, this molten rock (or lava) built up to form a submerged, cone-shaped peak called a seamount. Eventually, the heap of lava broke the ocean surface and became an island.

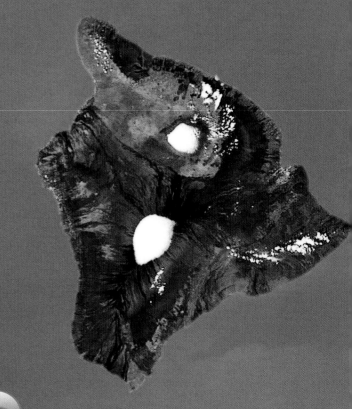

ISLANDS ON PLATE EDGES

Most oceanic islands lie along the edges where two tectonic plates meet. Where plates drift apart in mid-ocean, lava wells up to form an undersea ridge. The highest peaks may break the ocean's surface to form islands. In other places, ocean plates collide, and one slides below the other. The crust melts when it is underground and surges up to the ocean surface to form a line of islands.

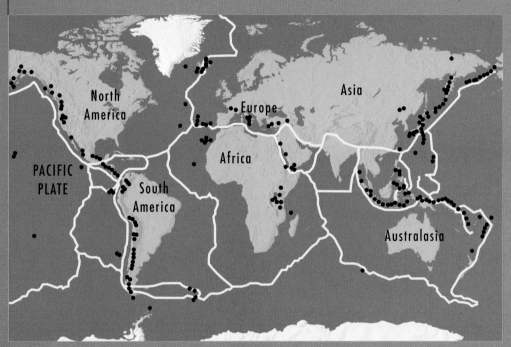

Coral islands

Coral reefs and islands are made of billions of skeletons! These are the chalky skeletons of very small sea creatures called coral polyps. These tiny animals thrive in the warm, shallow waters off of tropical islands. If a volcanic island later sinks or collapses, it leaves behind a hollow ring of coral called a coral atoll.

This coral island is one of the Maldive Islands off of southwest India. It formed around a mountain that later sank, leaving a ring-shaped atoll.

Climate and wildlife

Many islands have a mild, wet climate. This is because ocean breezes cool the island in the summer and warm it in the winter, while moist ocean winds bring rain. Many islands have unique plants and animals that are not found on the nearest mainland.

ISLAND HABITATS

Islands have different habitats, depending on whether they lie in tropical, temperate, or polar waters. The island's rock also affects the landscape, soil, and plants. Large islands may have a range of habitats. Madagascar is a big island off of Africa with rain forests, grasslands, dry scrublands, swamps, and coral reefs.

Remote islands are colonized by plant seeds carried by wind or water. This palm-tree seedling (left) is sprouting from a nut that washed up on a tropical lava beach.

UNUSUAL WILDLIFE

Remote islands often have an unusual mix of wildlife. Most animals found on oceanic islands arrived by either flying, floating, or swimming. For this reason, birds, bats, and insects are common, along with water-dwellers, such as seals and turtles. Land animals are much rarer. Once they have reached an island, plants and animals evolve (change slowly) to become new species that are better adapted to the conditions in their new environment.

Unique animals

Oceanic islands are often home to animals found nowhere else. For example, Madagascar is home to unique mammals called lemurs. These mammals resemble monkeys, but belong to another group of primates. The island also has hedgehoglike creatures called tenrecs, and a unique cat called the fossa.

Ring-tailed lemurs are one of 30 species of lemur found only on Madagascar.

How are islands used?

Many islands have rich natural resources such as fish, timber, and minerals. Land that can be farmed and settled is often the most precious resource of all. Since ancient times, islands have been settled by humans to make use of these resources.

Many islands in the tropics have large plantations. Crops such as bananas (below), tea, coffee, rubber, and sugar are grown for sale abroad.

SETTLEMENTS AND COLONIES

In prehistoric times, remote islands were colonized by seafaring peoples, such as the Polynesians of the South Pacific. These original settlers survived by fishing and farming. From the 1500s, European explorers reached and colonized many islands, claiming them for their own countries. Timber, minerals, and other resources were harvested and shipped back to Europe.

The islands of Japan have many large, modern cities, such as the port of Kobe, shown here.

NEW CHANGES

From the 1800s, industrialization brought huge changes to some islands. Small settlements grew into modern cities or busy ports with docks and factories. During the last half of the 1900s, tourism became a major industry on many islands. Jet airliners allowed people to fly to remote islands, and hotels spread along the shore.

Test sites

In the mid-1900s, some oceanic islands were used to test nuclear weapons. The remoteness of the islands made them seem a good choice for weapons tests. In the 1950s, the United States carried out bomb tests on the remote Pacific island of Bikini. Local people were forced to leave the island.

During the 1950s and 1960s, the United States exploded 70 nuclear bombs on Bikini and on another island, Enewetak.

13

Protecting islands

Islands are fragile environments where the balance of nature is easily upset. Activities such as fishing, farming, and mining can threaten local wildlife and damage precious habitats. Conservation is now a top priority on many islands.

WILDLIFE AT RISK

Hunting and fishing are often important industries on islands, but they also threaten animals such as seals, fish, and turtles. In some cases, they have caused extinctions, where species of animals disappear completely. On the Indian Ocean island of Mauritius, a flightless bird called the dodo was hunted to extinction in the 1500s. Tourism can also disturb island wildlife.

A tourist photographs a turtle that has come ashore to lay eggs. The breeding habits of these marine reptiles can be disturbed by the bright lights and noise of hotels and tourists.

THREATENED HABITATS

Island habitats are often harmed by farming, forestry, and mining. On many islands, forests have been stripped for timber. Native vegetation has been cleared to make way for farms, settlements, and sometimes mines. Fortunately, conservation is now a key issue on many islands. Wild habitats have been saved by the establishment of reserves and nature parks.

Phosphate mining is the main industry on Christmas Island in the Indian Ocean. Like farming and forestry, mining can lead to erosion and cause pollution.

Introducing wildlife

Island wildlife is also threatened when people introduce (bring in) new plants and animals. In the past, sailors often left goats and sheep on islands to provide food. These new animals stripped the local vegetation, leaving little for native plant-eaters. New predators, such as dogs, cats, and rats, also prey on island wildlife.

On the Caribbean island of Cuba, a unique mammal called the hutia has been hunted by introduced predators, such as rats and mongooses. Hutias are now very rare.

Arctic wilderness

Greenland

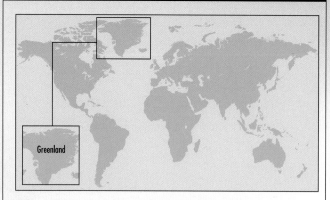

Greenland

STATISTICS

- Island type: Continental
- Size: 840,000 sq miles (2,175,000 sq km)
- Population: 56,344 (2007 estimate)
- Capital: Godthab (also known as Nuuk)
- National status: Self-governing province of Denmark
- Main industries: Fishing (also hunting and farming)

Greenland is the world's largest island, covering 840,000 square miles (2,175,000 square km). This continental island was once part of North America. Greenland's cold polar climate and scarce resources mean that relatively few people live there. Most of the island is an untouched wilderness, with a huge nature reserve in the northeast.

Greenland's Inuit people traditionally traveled in skin boats called kayaks (below), or in sleds pulled by dogs. Today, people also use aircraft and snowmobiles.

POPULATION

On Greenland, there are less than three people for every 38 square miles (100 square kilometers)! The original inhabitants were the Inuit, who arrived from North America about 5,000 years ago. Greenland became a colony of Denmark in the 1300s, but since 1979, the island has been self-governing. The Inuit traditionally live by fishing and hunting. Fishing is the main industry.

ICY CLIMATE

Much of Greenland lies inside the Arctic Circle. Temperatures range from 50°F (10°C) in the summer to -40°F (-40°C) in the winter. In the summer, the sun never sets, so it is light at midnight. In the winter, the sun never rises. Most of Greenland is covered by an ice cap 2 miles (3 km) deep.

The coasts of Greenland are warmed by the ocean, so their climate is milder than inland. Almost all of the island's inhabitants live in settlements on the southern coasts, where a little sheep farming is possible. Pictured below is the town of Kulusuk.

Viking colony

The Vikings were the first Europeans to settle on Greenland. In 985 CE, a Viking leader named Eric the Red landed on the island. Finding green pastures on the coast, Eric named the island Greenland. The Vikings survived on Greenland until the 1400s, when the climate grew colder and they abandoned their villages.

Viking sailors used this device, called a bearing dial, to navigate across the open ocean to Greenland.

Island evolution

Galápagos Islands

Galápagos Islands

STATISTICS

- Island type: Volcanic and oceanic
- Size: 3,029 sq miles (7,844 sq km)
- Population: 20,000 on four islands
- Largest town: Puerto Ayora, Isabela
- National status: Colony of Ecuador
- Main industries: Tourism

The Galápagos are a group of volcanic islands off of Ecuador in South America, famous for unique wildlife. In the 1830s, the British naturalist, Charles Darwin, visited the islands. The species he saw helped him to develop his ideas on evolution.

CLIMATE AND WILDLIFE

The Galápagos consist of 15 large islands and many small islets. The climate is quite dry. The islands lie on the equator, but are cooled by a cold ocean current. Unique wildlife includes a tropical penguin and the marine iguana—the world's only seagoing lizard. There are also giant tortoises.

HUMAN IMPACT

The Galápagos were discovered in the 1500s. Over the centuries, sailors landed on the islands to hunt for fresh meat, and this reduced seal and tortoise populations. Sailors also left goats, sheep, and pigs, which ate the vegetation. The Galápagos became a reserve in 1959, and park fees now help to pay for conservation work.

Galápagos tortoises are among the world's largest tortoises. They grow to 4 ft. (1.2 m) long and can weigh over 440 lbs. (200 kg).

Thirteen species of finch are found on the Galápagos. Some have stout beaks suitable for cracking seeds, and others have slender bills for catching insects.

Charles Darwin

Charles Darwin studied the wildlife of the Galápagos in 1835. He studied the 13 species of finch that live on the islands, and guessed that all 13 were descended from a single species. This species had spread to the other islands in the Galápagos and evolved beaks of different shapes to eat local foods.

Darwin's studies of Galápagos finches led him to develop his theory of evolution. He published his ideas in 1859.

Volcanic dangers

Santorini

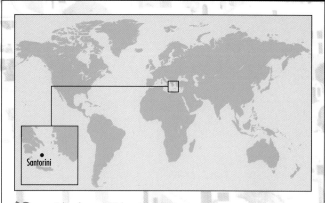

STATISTICS

- *Island type: Volcanic*
- *Size: 29 sq miles (73 sq km)*
- *Population: 11,000 (2002 estimate)*
- *Largest town: Phira*
- *National status: Part of Greece*
- *Main industries: Tourism, wine growing*

Volcanic islands are always at risk from fresh eruptions. People, plants, and animals can die if a volcano erupts, spouting red-hot lava and clouds of ash. About 3,500 years ago, an eruption on the Greek island of Santorini brought disaster to the ancient world.

ERUPTION

Around 2000 BCE, Santorini was an outpost of the Minoan Empire, based on the island of Crete to the south. In about 1600 BCE, Santorini's volcano exploded, showering ash far and wide. The explosion formed a huge hollow called a caldera, into which seawater gushed. This sent giant waves, called tsunamis, across the ocean. Ash engulfed the town of Akrotiri on Santorini, while cities on Crete were wrecked by giant waves.

This satellite view shows the main island of Santorini and smaller islands curving around a central bay. This deep bay is the caldera left by the explosion of 1600 BCE.

Steep cliffs overlook the deep bay, which is actually the caldera of the volcano. Visitors from ships docking in the bay have to climb the steep cliffs on donkeys or by cable car.

THE ISLAND TODAY

After 1500 BCE, Santorini became a colony of ancient Greece, Rome, and then the Ottoman Empire. In 1912, it became part of the modern state of Greece. The island now has about 11,000 inhabitants. Vines grow well in the volcanic soil, but water is scarce. The main industry on the island is tourism. Vacationers visit the ruins of Akrotiri, which have been excavated, or relax on beaches made of black volcanic sand.

Minoan civilization

The Minoans flourished on Crete from 3000 to 1100 BCE. The Minoan capital, Knossos, was the center of a mighty empire. The tsunamis of 1600 BCE wrecked coastal cities and broke the power of the Minoans. The disaster may also have inspired the legend of Atlantis, which tells of a beautiful island city under the sea.

The palace at Knossos has been partly restored. Beautiful wall paintings there show scenes from Minoan life.

Crowded city

Manhattan Island

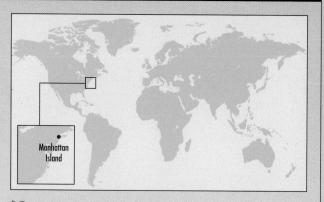

Manhattan Island

STATISTICS

- Island type: Continental
- Size: 23 sq miles (58 sq km)
- Population: 1,537,195 (2007 census)
- National status: Part of the United States
- Main industries: Finance, trade, manufacturing, service industries, tourism

Around the world, many islands are now intensively settled and developed—and none more so than Manhattan Island, which lies at the heart of New York City. Good transportation links are vital on crowded islands. Bridges, tunnels, and ferries connect Manhattan with other islands and the mainland.

This photograph shows Manhattan's docks around 1900. Later, the deepwater docks were moved to the mainland. New York is still among the world's 20 largest ports.

THE CITY RISES

Manhattan Island lies on a natural harbor at the mouths of the Hudson and East Rivers. In the 1620s, Dutch traders founded the first settlement on this small island. In the 1800s, large docks were built, and factories sprang up to process raw materials brought by boat. By 1900, one of the world's largest cities had spread to the surrounding mainland.

MODERN MANHATTAN

Over 1.5 million people now live on Manhattan Island. On working days, the city's population doubles as people commute here to work. Manhattan Island lies at the heart of America's business capital. It is also a major tourist destination. Visitors come to see Manhattan's parks, museums, and shops, and landmarks such as the Statue of Liberty.

On crowded islands, the only way to build is up! Manhattan bristles with tall skyscrapers. The Chrysler Building, with its graceful spire, is currently the city's second-tallest building after the Empire State Building.

Central Park

Manhattan's Central Park provides a much-needed green space in the heart of a bustling, polluted city. Covering 1.3 sq miles (3.4 sq km), the park was laid out in the 1850s. There are playgrounds, sports facilities, and two ice rinks. The park is especially peaceful when it is closed to traffic during the evening and at weekends.

A satellite view of Central Park's lakes, with the buildings of central New York City on either side.

Rich resources

New Guinea

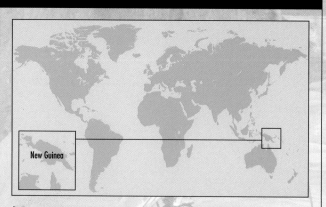

New Guinea

STATISTICS

- Island type: Continental
- Size: 320,000 sq miles (818,000 sq km)
- Population: 6.4 million (2000 estimate)
- Largest towns: Port Moresby (PNG), Jayapura (WNG)
- National status: Western New Guinea is part of Indonesia; Papua New Guinea is independent
- Main industries: Farming, forestry, mining

New Guinea in the western Pacific is the world's second-largest island. This landmass is divided between two nations. The western half, Western New Guinea, belongs to Indonesia. The eastern half, Papua New Guinea, is an independent country. The island's rich resources are as yet under-used, but this is changing fast.

LANDSCAPE AND FIRST SETTLERS

New Guinea is a very mountainous island. Lying just south of the equator, the low-lying coasts are hot and humid, but the mountains are cooler. Much of the island is covered with dense rain forests, which are home to birds of paradise. Tens of thousands of years ago, New Guinea was settled by Polynesians, who arrived in canoes.

New Guinea wildlife includes birds of paradise (left), tree kangaroos, large birds called cassowaries, and the world's largest butterfly, the Queen Alexandra birdwing.

Mining and other industries mean that New Guinea's forests are disappearing rapidly. Heavy rain washes away soil that is no longer held in place by tree roots. This is called erosion.

EXPLOITING RESOURCES

New Guinea's natural resources include forests of valuable hardwood. In some areas, huge tracts of forest have been felled. Western New Guinea has two large copper mines. Nickel, oil, and natural gas are also mined, causing pollution. Papua New Guinea was a colony of Britain, then Australia, before becoming independent in 1975. In 2006, Western New Guinea gained partial independence from Indonesia, but many people want full independence.

Village life

Until recently, about half of New Guinea's six million people lived in rural settlements. Villages in the mountains have round, thatched huts. In the lowlands, many houses are built on stilts, so they stand above any flooding. More and more people are now moving from inland villages to find work in coastal towns.

Until recently, the remote hill people of Papua New Guinea had little contact with the outside world. They survived by hunting, growing sweet potatoes, and raising pigs.

Threatened paradise

Maldives

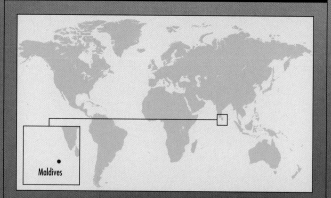

STATISTICS

- Island type: Coral atolls
- Size: 115 sq miles (298 sq km)
- Population: 369,031 (2006 estimate) on 200 islands
- Capital: Male
- National status: Independent republic
- Main industries: Tourism, fishing, farming

The Maldives are a group of coral islands in the Indian Ocean. About 1,200 small islands are grouped into a dozen atolls. White-sand beaches and blue lagoons make this an idyllic holiday destination. However, these low-lying islands are threatened by rising sea levels.

CORAL ISLANDS

The original settlers of the Maldives came from Sri Lanka, 435 miles (700 km) to the northeast. At various times, the islands belonged to Holland, Portugal, and Britain, before gaining independence in 1965. Fishing used to be the main industry but now it is tourism. Tourists are attracted by the stunning beaches and coral reefs.

Male, capital of the Maldives, has been heavily developed. Buildings include several mosques, where the islands' Muslim population worship.

A diver studies a beautiful but poisonous lionfish—just one of the many colorful species that can be seen on the Maldives' coral reefs.

RISING SEAS

The Maldives are extremely low-lying, with a maximum height of just 8 ft. (2.3 m) above sea level. Scientists believe sea levels are now rising worldwide because the Earth is getting warmer, as pollution from cars, factories, and power stations traps the sun's heat. The polar ice caps are melting, which is swelling the oceans and raising sea levels.

At risk from the waves

In the 1900s, sea levels rose by 8 in. (20 cm). If this process continues, much of the Maldives could be underwater by 2100. Another risk comes from large waves, or tsunamis. In 2004, tsunamis caused by an earthquake off of southeast Asia washed straight over some of the Maldives, causing extensive damage.

The Maldives were badly damaged by the 2004 tsunamis, even though the source of the waves was thousands of miles away.

Change and conservation

New Zealand

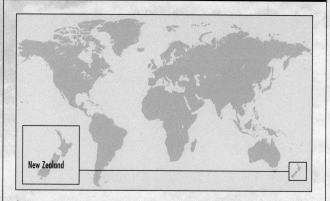

New Zealand

STATISTICS

- Island type: Continental, partly volcanic
- Size: 104,454 sq miles (270,534 sq km)
- Population: 4,115,771 (2007 estimate)
- Capital: Wellington (largest city: Auckland)
- National status: Independent nation
- Main industries: Farming, manufacturing, service industries

New Zealand, in the southwest Pacific, is known for its distinctive wildlife, including several species of flightless birds. In the last 200 years, however, these islands have been changed greatly by human settlement. Native wildlife is threatened, but conservation work is helping to repair the damage done.

HUMAN IMPACT

New Zealand's first settlers were a Polynesian people called the Maori, who arrived about 1,000 years ago. Europeans began to settle from the 1800s. New animals introduced by humans included dogs, cats, possums, and weasels, which preyed on defenseless island birds. The Europeans also brought sheep and cattle, and cleared forests to make pastures. All these changes threatened native wildlife, and some species became extinct.

Maori culture is thriving in New Zealand, unlike traditional ways on other islands. Maori meeting houses (left) are used for ceremonies and gatherings.

HABITATS AND WILDLIFE

New Zealand consists of two large islands and many smaller ones. The South Island is mainly mountainous with a cool climate, but the North Island is somewhat lower with milder conditions. Isolated from other landmasses for over 150 million years, New Zealand has many unique species, including flightless birds such as the kiwi. Scientists believe these island birds lost the ability to fly because they had very few predators.

Sheep farming is a major industry in New Zealand. However, these nonnative animals have caused widespread erosion as they strip the ground of plants that hold the soil in place.

Conserving rare animals

Conservationists are now working to preserve New Zealand's unique wildlife. Flightless birds and a rare reptile called the tuatara are protected on offshore island sanctuaries. Nonnative hunters, such as rats and weasels, have been carefully removed, so there is nothing to hunt these endangered animals.

Tuataras are very unusual reptiles that resemble lizards. They grow to 8 in. (20 cm) long and can live for 100 years.

Glossary, Further Information, and Web Sites

ARCHIPELAGO
A large group of islands scattered over a wide expanse of ocean.

ATOLL
An island made of coral, often in the form of a ring surrounding a lagoon.

BARRIER ISLAND
An island made of sediment dropped by water currents.

CALDERA
A hollow that forms when a volcano's cone collapses.

CAUSEWAY
A thin strip of land linking an island to the mainland. It may flood at high tide.

COLONIZE
When people, plants, or animals reach and settle on a place such as an island.

CONSERVATION
Work done in order to protect nature.

CONTINENTAL SHELF
A broad ledge that surrounds a continent, forming a shelf of shallow water.

EROSION
The wearing away of the land by wind, water, or ice.

EVOLVE
When species of living things change slowly to suit their environment.

EXPLOIT
To make full use of a resource, sometimes at the risk of damage to the environment.

EXTINCTION
When a whole species dies out.

HABITAT
A particular place where plants and animals live, such as a forest or a desert.

HOT SPOT
A weak point near the center of a tectonic plate, where molten rock bursts through to form volcanoes.

ICE AGE
A period in the Earth's history when ice covered more land than it does today.

ISLET
A tiny island.

LAGOON
A shallow coastal lake.

LAVA
Hot, molten rock that erupts from a volcano.

NATIVE
The original plants, animals, or people found on an island.

POLAR
To do with the North and South Poles.

PRIMATE
A member of the group of mammals that includes apes, monkeys, and humans.

RING OF FIRE
A ring of volcanoes that runs around the edge of the Pacific Ocean.

SEAMOUNT
An undersea mountain, formed by volcanic activity.

SEDIMENT
Loose particles of rocky material, such as sand or mud.

TECTONIC PLATE
One of the huge, rigid plates that make up the outer layer of the Earth.

TEMPERATE
To do with the regions between the tropics and the poles.

TROPICAL
To do with the regions that lie on either side of the equator.

FURTHER READING

Earth's Changing Islands
by Neil Morris
(Raintree Steck-Vaughn, 2003)

The World's Top Ten: Islands
by Neil Morris
(Raintree Steck-Vaughn, 1997)

WEB SITES

Due to the changing nature of Internet links, PowerKids Press has developed an online list of Web sites related to the subject of this book. This site is updated regularly. Please use this link to access this list:
www.powerkidslinks.com/geon/island

Islands topic web

Use this topic web to discover themes and ideas in subjects that are related to islands.

GEOGRAPHY
- The formation of oceanic, continental, and barrier islands.
- How coral reefs form.
- How plate tectonics and volcanic activity can shape islands.
- The natural resources found on islands.

SCIENCE AND THE ENVIRONMENT
- How plants and animals colonize islands.
- Evolution of island wildlife.
- Impact of people on island environments and conservation work.

MATHS AND ECONOMICS
- Calculating the density of island populations, using statistics on island size and population.
- Exploitation of island resources, both in the past and today.

ISLANDS

ENGLISH AND LITERACY
- Stories, myths, and legends about islands.
- First-hand accounts of modern life on islands by people who live there.
- Debate the pros and cons of tourist development on remote tropical islands.

HISTORY
- The history of exploration and the discovery of various islands.
- Colonization of islands and the gaining of independence.
- Strategic importance of islands for trade and military use.

Index